I0479957

Riding the Wave

How to Capitalize on the Latest Trends in Business, Marketing, and More

by

Helen B. Peart

TABLE OF CONTENT

Introduction

In today's fast-paced business landscape, staying ahead of emerging trends is more important than ever. Whether you're an entrepreneur starting a new business, a marketer looking to expand your reach, or a seasoned business owner looking to stay competitive, understanding the latest trends and adapting your business to take advantage of them is essential for success.

In this book, we'll explore how to capitalize on the latest trends in business, marketing, and more. We'll discuss strategies for identifying emerging trends, adapting your business to take advantage of them, measuring success, and staying ahead of the curve.

Whether you're a startup or a well-established business, these strategies can help you stay competitive and achieve long-term success in a rapidly changing market.

Throughout this book, we'll cover a range of topics, including:

· The importance of staying up-to-date on the latest trends

· Strategies for identifying emerging trends in business and marketing

· How to adapt your business to take advantage of emerging trends

· Measuring success and staying ahead of emerging trends

· Staying creative and innovative to capitalize on emerging trends

By the end of this book, you'll better understand how to stay ahead of emerging trends and position your business for success. Whether you're looking to expand your customer base, improve your products or services, or stay competitive in a rapidly changing market, the strategies outlined in this book can help you achieve your goals. So let's dive in and start riding the wave of emerging trends!

Chapter 1

Why Trends Matter for Your Business

Trends are everywhere. From fashion and entertainment to technology and business, trends shape how we live, work, and consume. For businesses, understanding trends is essential to staying relevant and competitive in today's fast-paced market.

This chapter will explore why trends matter for your business and how you can use them to your advantage.

Why Trends Matter

Trends are more than just fleeting fads or passing crazes. They represent larger shifts in consumer behavior, preferences, and expectations.

By understanding and leveraging these shifts, businesses can gain a competitive edge and drive growth.

Here are some of the key reasons why trends matter for your business:

Identify new opportunities: Trends can reveal new market segments, product ideas, or business models that were previously overlooked. By keeping an eye on emerging trends, you can spot opportunities for growth and innovation.

Stay relevant: Trends reflect what's current and in demand. By incorporating relevant trends into your business strategy, you can stay relevant and top-of-mind with your customers.

Differentiate your brand: By capitalizing on unique or emerging trends, you can differentiate your brand from competitors and stand out in a crowded market.

Increase customer engagement: Trends can be a powerful way to connect with customers and build engagement. You can tap into customers' interests and preferences by aligning your business with relevant trends.

How to Identify Trends

Identifying trends can seem daunting, but it doesn't have to be. Here are a few tips for spotting emerging trends:

Monitor social media: Social media platforms are a goldmine for spotting emerging trends.

Keep an eye on hashtags, popular posts, and influencers to stay up-to-date on what's trending.

Follow industry publications: Industry publications, such as trade magazines and blogs, are a great source of information on emerging trends in your specific industry.

Conduct customer research: Conducting surveys, focus groups, or online polls can help you gather insights into customer preferences and identify emerging trends.

Attend trade shows and conferences: Attending trade shows and conferences in your industry can help you stay up-to-date on the latest trends and innovations.

Conclusion

This chapter explores why trends matter for your business and how you can identify them. Stay current with emerging trends, spot new opportunities, differentiate your brand, and increase customer engagement. In the next chapter, we'll dive deeper into how to evaluate trends and determine which ones are worth pursuing your business.

Chapter 2

Evaluating Trends

How to Determine Which Ones Are Worth Pursuing

Identifying emerging trends is just the first step. Once you've identified a trend, you must evaluate whether it's worth pursuing your business. This chapter will explore how to evaluate trends and determine which ones are worth pursuing.

Factors to Consider When Evaluating Trends

Not all trends are created equal. Some may be a fad, while others have the potential to shape entire industries. When evaluating trends, consider the following factors:

Relevance to your business: Is the trend relevant to your industry, target market, and business model? If not, it may not be worth pursuing.

Sustainability: Is the trend likely to last, or is it a short-term fad? Trends that have staying power are more likely to be worth pursuing.

Potential impact: What is the trend's potential impact on your business? Will it help you grow, differentiate your brand, or solve a specific problem?

Competitive landscape: How are your competitors responding to the trend? Is there an opportunity to differentiate your brand and stand out?

Resources required: What resources will you need to pursue the trend? Can you allocate time, money, and personnel to capitalize on the trend?

Examples of Businesses That Have Successfully Evaluated Trends

Here are a few examples of businesses that have successfully evaluated and capitalized on emerging trends:

Netflix: When Netflix first launched, it was a DVD-by-mail service. But as streaming technology emerged as a trend, Netflix quickly pivoted its business model to focus on streaming video content. Today, Netflix is the world's leading streaming service, with over 200 million subscribers worldwide.

Tesla: Tesla has been at the forefront of the trend toward electric vehicles. By betting on the trend toward sustainability and renewable energy, Tesla has positioned itself as a leader in the automotive industry and has seen impressive growth.

Dollar Shave Club: Dollar Shave Club capitalized on the trend toward subscription-based services and disrupted the traditional razor market. Dollar Shave Club built a loyal customer base by offering a low-cost subscription service for high-quality razors. Unilever eventually acquired it for $1 billion.

Conclusion
This chapter explored evaluating trends and determining which ones are worth pursuing your business. By considering factors like relevance, sustainability, potential impact, competitive landscape, and resource requirements, you can

decide which trends to pursue. The next chapter will explore strategies for adapting your business to take advantage of emerging trends.

Chapter 3

Adapting Your Business to Emerging Trends

Once you've identified and evaluated a trend, the next step is to adapt your business to take advantage of it. This chapter will explore strategies for adapting your business to emerging trends.

1. Update Your Business Strategy

You may need to update your business strategy to capitalize on emerging trends. This could include:

· Reevaluating your target market and adjusting your marketing messaging to align with the trend

· Rethinking your product or service offerings to incorporate the trend

· Exploring new business models that align with the trend

Updating your business strategy to reflect emerging trends allows you to position your business for growth and success.

2. Invest in Technology

Many emerging trends are driven by new technology. You may need to invest in new technology to capitalize on these trends. This could include:

· Adopting new software or tools to improve your operations or customer experience

· Exploring new marketing channels, such as social media or influencer marketing

· Implementing new payment or checkout technologies, such as mobile payments or contactless payments.

By investing in technology that aligns with emerging trends, you can stay ahead of the curve and provide your customers with a better experience.

3. Foster a Culture of Innovation

To stay competitive in a rapidly changing market, fostering a culture of innovation within your business is important. This could include:

· Encouraging experimentation and risk-taking

· Providing resources and support for employees to pursue new ideas

· Celebrating successes and learning from failures.

By fostering a culture of innovation, you can stay agile and adaptable in the face of emerging trends.

4. Collaborate and Network

Collaborating and networking with other businesses and industry experts can help you stay on top of emerging trends.

This could include:

· Joining industry associations or trade groups

· Attending conferences and events in your industry

· Forming partnerships or collaborations with other businesses that are also capitalizing on the trend.

By collaborating and networking with others in your industry, you can gain new insights and ideas for adapting your business to emerging trends.

Conclusion

In this chapter, we've explored strategies for adapting your business to emerging trends. By updating your business strategy, investing in technology, fostering a culture of innovation, and collaborating and networking with others in your industry, you can position your business for growth and success.

In the next chapter, we'll explore how to measure the success of your efforts to capitalize on emerging trends.

Chapter 4

Measuring Success in Trend-Driven

Marketing

Once you've adapted your business to capitalize on emerging trends, the next step is to measure the success of your efforts. This chapter will explore how to measure success in trend-driven marketing.

1. Set Clear Goals and KPIs

Before measuring success, you must set clear goals and key performance indicators (KPIs). This could include:

· Increasing website traffic or social media followers

· Generating leads or sales

· Improving customer engagement or satisfaction

Setting clear goals and KPIs allows you to measure progress and adjust your strategy as needed.

2. Use Data and Analytics

Data and analytics can provide valuable insights into the success of your trend-driven marketing efforts. This could include:

· Tracking website and social media metrics, such as clicks, impressions, and engagement

· Analyzing customer data, such as demographics and behavior

· Monitoring sales and revenue

Using data and analytics, you can identify areas of strength and weakness in your trend-driven marketing strategy.

3. Monitor Industry Trends

As trends continue to evolve, it's important to stay up-to-date and monitor industry trends. This could include:

· Keeping an eye on social media trends and hashtags

· Monitoring industry news and publications

· Following thought leaders and influencers in your industry

You can adjust your strategy by monitoring industry trends to stay relevant and capitalize on new opportunities.

4. Test and Experiment

Finally, testing and experimentation can help you fine-tune your trend-driven marketing strategy. This could include:

· A/B testing different marketing messages or tactics

· Experimenting with new technologies or platforms

· Conducting customer surveys or focus groups to gather feedback

By testing and experimenting, you can identify what works and what doesn't in your trend-driven marketing strategy.

Conclusion

In this chapter, we've explored how to measure success in trend-driven marketing. By setting clear goals and KPIs, using data and analytics, monitoring industry trends, and testing and experimenting, you can measure the success of your trend-driven marketing efforts and adjust your strategy as needed. In the next chapter, we'll explore how to stay ahead of emerging trends and maintain a competitive edge in your industry.

Chapter 5

Staying Ahead of Emerging Trends

As trends continue to evolve, staying ahead of the curve and maintaining a competitive edge in your industry is important. This chapter will explore strategies for staying ahead of emerging trends.

1. Keep an Eye on Emerging Technologies
Emerging technologies are often the driving force behind new trends. By keeping an eye on emerging technologies, you can identify new trends early and start planning how to adapt your business to take advantage of them.
2. Follow Industry Thought Leaders and Influencers

The following industry thought leaders and influencers could also help you stay ahead of emerging trends. This could include:

· Following industry leaders on social media or subscribing to their blogs or newsletters

· Attending industry conferences or events where thought leaders and influencers will be speaking

· Forming relationships with thought leaders and influencers in your industry.

By following industry thought leaders and influencers, you can gain new insights and ideas for adapting your business to emerging trends.

1. Encourage Employee Innovation

Encouraging innovation among your employees can also help you stay ahead of emerging trends. This could include:

· Providing resources and support for employees to pursue new ideas and projects

· Offering incentives or recognition for successful innovation

· Creating a culture of innovation and experimentation within your organization

By encouraging employee innovation, you can tap into your team's collective creativity and stay agile and adaptable in the face of emerging trends.

1. Conduct Market Research

Conducting market research can also help you stay ahead of emerging trends. This could include:

· Surveying customers and prospects to identify emerging needs and preferences

· Conducting focus groups or user testing to gather feedback on new products or services

· Monitoring competitor activity to identify emerging trends in your industry

By conducting market research, you can better understand your target market and identify emerging trends before they become mainstream.

Conclusion

In this chapter, we've explored strategies for staying ahead of emerging trends. By keeping an eye on emerging technologies, following industry thought leaders and influencers, encouraging employee innovation, and conducting market research, you can position your business for success in a rapidly changing market. In the final chapter, we'll summarize key takeaways from this ebook and offer final thoughts on capitalizing on emerging trends.

Chapter 6

Final Thoughts on Capitalizing on

Emerging Trends

In this book, we've explored how to capitalize on emerging trends in business, marketing, and more. We've discussed the importance of staying up-to-date on the latest trends, adapting your business to take advantage of them, measuring success, and staying ahead of emerging trends. This final chapter will summarize key takeaways and offer final thoughts on capitalizing on emerging trends.

1. Be Agile and Adaptable

One of the key themes throughout this book is the importance of being agile and adaptable in the face of emerging trends. The business landscape is constantly changing, and businesses that need to adapt faster must catch up. By staying up-to-date on the latest trends, being willing to experiment and innovate, and constantly re-evaluating your strategy, you can stay ahead of the curve and maintain a competitive edge.

2. Embrace Technology

Technology is often the driving force behind emerging trends, and businesses that embrace technology are more likely to succeed in a rapidly changing market. Whether leveraging AI and machine learning to automate processes, using social media to connect with customers, or adopting new technologies to improve products or services, businesses that embrace technology are more likely to stay ahead of the curve.

3. Focus on Customer Needs

Ultimately, your business's success depends on meeting customers' needs and preferences. By staying attuned to emerging customer needs and preferences, you can identify new trends early and adapt your business to meet those needs. Whether conducting market research, monitoring social media trends, or paying attention to customer feedback, focusing on customer needs is key to capitalizing on emerging trends.

4. Stay Creative and Innovative

Finally, staying creative and innovative is essential to capitalizing on emerging trends. Whether experimenting with new marketing tactics, developing new products or services, or simply thinking outside the box, businesses willing to take risks and try new things are more likely to succeed in a rapidly changing market.

Conclusion

In conclusion, staying ahead of emerging trends is essential for businesses to maintain a competitive edge in a rapidly changing market. By keeping up-to-date on the latest trends, adapting your business to take advantage of them, measuring success, and staying ahead of emerging trends, you can position your business for success.

Throughout this book, we've explored a range of strategies for capitalizing on emerging trends, including identifying and adapting your business to take advantage of them, measuring success, staying ahead of emerging trends, and staying creative and innovative.

By following these strategies, businesses can stay agile and adaptable, embrace technology, focus on customer needs, and remain competitive. However, it's important to remember that there is no one-size-fits-all approach to capitalizing on emerging trends. Every business is different, and what works for one business may not work for another. The key is to stay attuned to the needs and preferences of your target market, experiment with new ideas and strategies, and be willing to adapt and evolve.

By proactively identifying and capitalizing on emerging trends, businesses can position themselves for long-term success in a rapidly changing market. Whether it's through leveraging new technologies, adapting products and services to meet emerging needs, or simply staying creative and innovative, businesses that stay ahead of the curve are more likely to thrive in the years to come.

www.ingramcontent.com/pod-product-compliance
Lightning Source LLC
Chambersburg PA
CBHW070751220526
45467CB00018B/2055